Into the Wilderness

Sarah York

The Apollo Ranch Institute Press

Printed in U.S.A.

Text design by Suzanne Morgan
Cover design by Bruce Jones
Cover illustration by Laura Huff

Excerpt from poem #501, "This World Is Not Conclusion," by Emily Dickinson reprinted by permission of the publishers and the Trustees of Amherst College from *The Poems of Emily Dickinson*, Thomas Johnson, ed., Cambridge, Mass.: The Belknap Press of Harvard University Press, Copyright 1951, © 1955, 1979, 1983 by the President and Fellows of Harvard College.

Excerpt from "Little Gidding" in *Four Quartets*, copyright 1943 by T.S. Eliot and renewed 1971 by Esme Valerie Eliot, reprinted by permission of Harcourt Brace Jovanovich, Inc.

York, Sarah
    Into the wilderness / Sarah York.
        p. cm
    ISBN 0-9679058-0-X
    1. Spirituality and inspiration—English. 2. Lent—
Meditations and reflections—English.
I. Title.
BV85.C35 2000
242'.34—dc2   00-191108

To the members and friends of the
First Universalist Church
of Southold, New York, and the
Unitarian Church of Rockville, Maryland

Contents

When Jesus was baptized the spirit descended upon him like a dove and God said, "This is my son, in whom I am well pleased." It must have been a great feeling, but it didn't last long. The next thing Jesus knew, the nice spirit that had descended like a dove became aggressive and *drove* him into the wilderness. There he spent forty days of deprivation, self-examination, and confrontation with the devil. This was no Sierra Club hike through the Qumran National Forest. He suffered; he struggled; he was tested. Jesus' solitary struggles to remain true to his covenant and calling echo those of his ancestors, who spent forty years in the wilderness establishing a religious community.

Wilderness is a part of every person's soul-journey, and part of our journey together as human beings who seek to live in community. Time in the wilderness is always a time of struggle. It is also a time of transformation and renewal. In traditional terms, it is a time of purification. The journey into wilderness reminds us that we are alone and not alone. We are neither where we have been nor where we are going. There is danger and possibility, risk and promise. In the wilderness, the spirit may descend like a dove and lift us on its wings of hope, then drive us into the depths of despair; it may affirm us with a gift of grace, then challenge us to change. In the stories and rituals of Eastern as well as Western religions, a journey into the wilderness represents a time when we both pursue and resist the Holy.

We may choose to enter the wilderness like the people of Yahweh, to escape bondage, or, like Henry David Thoreau, to "live deliberately." Or we may, like Jesus, be driven there without much choice. Once there, even our markers of time and space collapse, for this wilderness is not in space or time, but is the boundless territory of the soul.

Invocation Spirit of holiness, speak now to us.

Speak in the language of tradition, in words from scripture and poetry, in myths that capture the holy;

Speak in the language of faces—faces that tell of pain or longing or fear or joy or contentment or hope.

Speak to us in the language of music, with voices and rhythms that vibrate through body and soul;

Speak to us, holy mystery of the universe, in the language of winter—with beauty of austerity; and in the language of early spring—with buds bursting boldly into frost-threatened air.

Speak in the language of color, the language of form, the language of motion, the language of stillness.

And help us, please help us, to listen. Help us to hear the many languages that speak to us of our own possibility within the impossibility of life.

Amen.

Teach us to care and not to care
Teach us to sit still.
                    —T.S. Eliot

I thought Ash Wednesday was the title of a poem by T.S. Eliot until I learned about the liturgical year in divinity school. One day I had a chance to learn more about Ash Wednesday.

It was a very, very busy day. I arose at 5:00 a.m. to catch a train from Southold, on the eastern tip of Long Island, into New York City, where I was scheduled to tape a television interview. A ministers' meeting was to follow the taping, then I would rush back out to Southold to meet with the Religious Education Committee.

Oh, my, was I busy! And important. It isn't every day, after all, that one gets to be on television. But I kept thinking of the rabbit in *Alice in Wonderland* who scurries around looking at his pocket watch, saying, "I'm late, I'm late, for a very important date."

After we taped the program, two of my colleagues and I left the CBS studio to make our way to the Community Church, where we were late for the ministers' meeting. As we bustled through the subway and the crowded streets, weaving around less hurried pedestrians, I realized that it was Ash Wednesday. I was reminded by the sign on the foreheads of many who passed us. What looked like a smudge of dirt was the sign of the cross made with ashes from palms blessed the previous year on Palm Sunday. I recalled not only what I knew of how the ashes are used, but also the verse from Genesis that is recited to each person as the ashes are rubbed on the forehead: "Remember . . . thou art dust, and to dust thou shalt return." Every time I passed someone with a smudgy face, I would hear the verse again: "Thou art dust and to dust thou shalt return."

I slowed my pace, lagging behind my companions, and paused to reflect that I was dust, already late for a very important date.

Season of Mud   A friend of mine from Maine says that down east there are five seasons: summer, fall, winter, spring, and mud. Mud is the season between winter and spring, the season of melting snow when winter's icy grip loosens its hold . . . but doesn't quite let go.

When I lived near the bay that divides the eastern end of Long Island into two forks, I witnessed the beginning of this fifth season in a phenomenon which Thoreau describes as the "thundering" of the ice. Dressed for insulation from the February wind, I walked on the snow-covered beach. A sharp cracking sound boomed from beneath the frozen stillness of the bay's surface. I marveled with Thoreau: "Who," he asks, "would have suspected so large and thick-skinned a thing to be so sensitive?" The beach resembled an arctic glacier, large chunks of ice reflecting both sun and sky. They imposed a barrier between sand and sea that appeared invincible even though it was disappearing every moment. Many white ice-rafts drifted with the current while a flock of ducks squawked noisily above.

Two weeks later only a remnant of the imposing glacier remained, and the shoreline was visible again. I could stroll along a thin strip of sand between the water and the ice. I thought of the paradoxes of this in-between season when the rigid is juxtaposed with the fluid; when spring's warmth softens the winter earth and winter's chill snatches back the spring air; when each day is an unpredictable and unreliable combination of what was and what will be.

The season of mud begins with thunder and announces change; it is the season of transition. Transitions are times when the thick skin of habit that protected us surrenders to the possibilities of growth and renewal. The inner thawing renders us sensitive and vulnerable to the unpredictable, until we emerge comfortably into new ways of being. We aren't sure who we are or where we will end up.

In the midst of the mud and muddle of all transitions, the seeds of promise stir quietly beneath the surface like spring bulbs drinking the snow.

The Lesson of the Deer

We shall not cease from exploration,
And the end of all our exploring
Will be to arrive where we started
And know the place for the first time.
　　　　—T. S. Eliot, "Little Gidding"

I went to the woods because, like Thoreau, I wanted to "live deep and suck out all the marrow of life." On the final morning of my sojourn, four deer tiptoed across the clearing in front of my cabin, then disappeared into the trees. I tiptoed into the woods to catch another glimpse of these lovely animals. Unrewarded, I returned to the house. As I approached, the frightened deer looked up from the clearing for a moment before they darted silently into the trees once again. If only I had stayed!

We learn the lesson of the deer over and over. Off we go in pursuit of our dreams, only to find that what we wanted was in front of us all along. I wonder how many times we search far away for what is at home before we stay and receive it. I wonder how many times we look outside of ourselves for fulfillment before we realize that it is inside. Perhaps this lesson is one we always know, but never really learn.

Two boxes of Girl Scout cookies arrived.

"Why did you buy *two* boxes?" my husband asked.

"Because there were *two* children selling them," I replied.

When I bite into one of those delicious cookies, I remember the time in fifth grade that I peddled cookies with my best friend. In those days, we just took the boxes out and sold them—no orders. We stopped off to rest, and devoured an entire box of cookies. I understand why they take orders now.

I remember some of the things I learned as a Girl Scout—how to make my own stove out of cardboard and wax and a tuna can. How to tie three sticks together to hold a bowl of water. And how to choose a site for a latrine . . . and how to make the latrine.

Then there were the badges. One I earned for learning how to grow something from seed. With my mother's help, I chose nasturtiums. I remember the day I planted them, the day I saw the first sprouts, the day buds appeared . . . and the day that I noticed that they had withered from neglect.

I also earned the cooking badge. "Keep the fire low and turn the bacon frequently," my mother said. I tried that for a few minutes, then lost patience and turned the fire up. When I received the badge, there were still scars where the grease had attacked my arm. Withered flowers, burned bacon, and all . . . I still got the badges. That's because what we learn in the process is always more important than the way things come out.

Window or Aisle?   "Window or aisle?" the man at the counter asked as I
prepared to board the plane for Detroit.

No matter how often I fly, I always pause to make the
choice: To take a window seat means being able to get
a God's eye view of earth. But what if I want to go to the
restroom? It's such a bother to have to ask people to
move. And I don't like feeling trapped.

My answer is always the same: "Window." To choose
the window is to choose to see. Whether I am identify-
ing a river or marveling at the play of moonlight on the
ocean; whether the view is a patchwork of planted
fields, a city showing off its neon finery, or a comforter
of clouds, I am filled with a deep sense of awe. Sometimes, as the plane moves through a storm, breaking
through the clouds and into the sun, my own spirit
opens up to invite in the expanse of beauty. There is
always something to see—always something I have
never seen before.

Knowing that to choose the window is an invitation to
beauty, awe, and wonder—that it is even an opportu-
nity to break through the cloudiness of my own spirit—
why do I always pause to make the decision? Each time
we get a seat on a plane we are invited to choose to be
touched by the world or to remain complacent and take
it for granted. We are invited to choose beauty or fear,
vision or convenience. Each day of our lives, in fact, we
are given the choice, "Window or aisle?" Something
inside me will always pause before I choose . . . but I
think I'll take the window.

Give us the spirit of the child

Give us the child who lives within—
  —the child who trusts,
  —the child who imagines,
  —the child who sings,
  —the child who receives without reservation,
  —the child who gives without judgment.

Give us a child's eyes, that we may receive the beauty and freshness of this day like a sunrise;

Give us a child's ears, that we may hear the music of mythical times;

Give us a child's heart, that we may be filled with wonder and delight;

Give us a child's faith, that we may be cured of our cynicism;

Give us the spirit of the child, who is not afraid to need; who is not afraid to love.

Amen.

Between Night and Day

We must learn to reawaken and keep ourselves awake, not by mechanical aids, but by an infinite expectation of the dawn.

—Henry David Thoreau

Thoreau recognized a special power in the image of the dawn, which "contains an earlier, more sacred and auroral hour" and an invitation to awaken to "a poetic or divine life." In its not-asleep-yet-not-quite-awake quality, the dawn suspended him in a spirit of awakening and regeneration.

How few mornings do I experience dawn's awakening. Instead of a mechanical device, the cold nose of an impatient dog interrupts my sleep. Then the "Today Show" announces the news and weather and the daily routine begins. Occasionally when I get out for an early jog, I do awaken to the power of dawn. The air is still; a layer of steam rolls over the glassy water of a nearby lake; congregations of geese chatter in a mystical cacophony. The sky is shaded with subtle pinks and blues—lovely, but not spectacular—and sometimes a star or a sliver of moon lingers from the night.

If I try to name the special power of dawn, I come up with words like stillness, silence, creativity, possibility, renewal. When the day awakes and we awaken, we move through a fuzzy transitional time. We may not be certain where we are or what day it is—we are suspended in time and space. If we awaken naturally, as Thoreau urges, we are conscious of having been in another world—in our dreaming selves. Thoreau calls this other world the "infinite mind." Dawn, he says, is a time when the will is still asleep and "the mind works like a machine without friction."

Somewhere between night and day there is a time—a consciousness—when we can look at the sun and the moon and the stars all at once and connect with "an earlier, more sacred and auroral hour." Dawn is sacred time. Usually we sleep through it.

I went at sundown to the top of Dr. Ripley's hill and renewed my vows to the Genius of that place. Somewhat of awe, somewhat grand and solemn mingles with the beauty that shines afar around. In the West, where the sun was sinking behind the clouds, one pit of splendour lay as in a desert of space—a deposit of still light, not radiant.
—Ralph Waldo Emerson

Between Day and Night

One fall evening I went for a walk along a New England country path that opened onto a meadow, then wound along the edge of a lake, into the woods, and through rolling hills and farms. It was dusk and I bathed in the silence and stillness of the hour. The lake, though steamy in the morning, now reflected the golden trees, the falling leaves, and the changing colors of sunset. I paused to consider how the mood was different from the mood of dawn. The words that came to mind were "silence" and "stillness"—but a different stillness than that of the dawn. This was a stillness of peace, calm, enchantment, and mystery. I understood Emerson when he says, "Yet sweet and native as all those fair impressions on that summit fall on the eye and ear, they are not yet mine."

Between day and night we can look at the sun and the moon and the stars together, just as we can between night and day. At dusk, however, we are more conscious of being what Emerson calls "a stranger in nature." Dawn is our time of promise and self-reliance; dusk reminds us that for all of our knowledge of light and dark, we live in mystery.

Equinox   May we walk into day with knowledge of the night
And into night with knowledge of the dawn.

In my first year of ministry I received a request from a colleague that I lead a workshop for ministers on time management. My immediate response was, "You've got to be kidding! Me do a workshop on time management? You're talking to someone who puts in fifteen hours on a sermon between noon Saturday and 11:00 a.m. Sunday—*after* I've done the research."

I said no to doing the workshop, but for the wrong reason. I thought I should have it together before presuming to speak to colleagues. Then I realized that if I waited until I had it together before I ever preached on a sermon topic, we would be doing a lot of hymns and responsive readings on Sunday mornings.

It's a common misconception that strong people have it together and help those who aren't so strong. But how many people do you know who are so together that they don't need to reach out for help? If you know anyone like that, you probably don't like them very much. If they don't have any weaknesses, they can't understand yours very well.

And understanding is what we want from each other. Strength emerges when we know our own weakness. This is nothing new. But it doesn't hurt to remind ourselves from time to time that it's all right to be human.

Return to Chaos   I looked out the window, surprised to see winter's first snowfall. I wasn't ready.

"Have you seen my boots anywhere?" I asked my husband Chuck, after I had searched for them in every logical location in the house.

Forty-five minutes of climbing over boxes in the attic ("Here's the Christmas wrapping we couldn't find last week"), rummaging through closets ("I've looked there twice already, but you can go ahead and look anyway") and sneezing into the dust under beds ("Where did all *this* come from?") yielded only frustration. No boots.

It was Chuck who finally found the boots. I had given up after six trips to the attic, two trips to the basement, and multiple closet checks. The terrible truth is that they were in the attic in a box labeled "Camping Equipment," well hidden underneath a tent and a Coleman stove.

The fact is, we humans do not like to live in the kind of disorder where winter boots can get lost in a box of camping equipment. We are particularly uncomfortable when such disorder originates in our own minds.

But there it is, the terrible truth—or half of it, anyway. The other half is that once such a lapse of logic has taken place, a *return* to disorder is the only avenue of correction. It was only because Chuck could imagine the most illogical location for the boots that he could discover them.

Logic is useful, most of the time. But sometimes a return to chaos has its logic, too.

Where your treasure is, there will be your heart also.
                                —Luke 12:34

I had just graduated from divinity school, was newly ordained, and had accepted the call to my first church, on Long Island.

Chuck and I packed our possessions in a hired moving van. We sat on the front steps and watched the movers drive down the street and out of sight. It was an uneasy feeling. The next day we left for a week in Maine, where we would be before heading to our new home. That evening I called a church leader to be sure everything had arrived safely. There was an awkward silence, then she said, "Didn't the woman from the moving company get you? Didn't she tell you about the fire?"

I got a sick feeling in the pit of my stomach.

A week later we found out that a fire had consumed a warehouse and burned the back of our van, but it had destroyed very little that we truly valued. During that week, however, we suffered a prolonged anxiety attack.

When we finally unpacked and cleaned up the smoke damage, it was with a new appreciation for our paintings and sculptures and books—things we had collected for more than fifteen years, many of them family treasures. We had a new awareness that we were attached to some things, even to some things we did not need. During that week, however, as we took mental inventory of which things truly mattered, we came up with a surprisingly short list. We realized that we were not inordinately attached to what we had. We realized that we had a lot more than we really needed. We paused to consider how very rich we were without anything that was on that truck.

Then we put in our first request to the Church Building and Grounds Committee—for smoke alarms in the parsonage.

Love Contest   My husband called from England. "I miss you," he said.

"I miss you, too," I answered.

"But I miss you more than you miss me," he said.

"No," I came back, "I think I miss you more."

"But you're at home, with the church and friends," he said, "and I'm in a strange hotel. I miss you more."

"No," I argued, "I'm here at home with all the responsibility for the kids and the laundry and the housecleaning. . . . I miss you more."

And so we argued, each of us defining our missing in terms of our own need, until we decided that only the telephone company would benefit from our little love contest.

In more recent years I have realized that we sometimes don't really miss each other and may feel guilty about it, while other times we do miss each other and still need to be apart. Most importantly, missing isn't always connected with physical presence. We can be absent while we are together or together while we are absent. We need to be together. We need to be apart. Our separate needs do not always coincide.

Once when I was in the mountains for some time apart, I sat on the porch reflecting upon the human needs for individual growth and relationship. At the same time I noticed some things in the front yard. The wisteria I had cut back the previous year was winding its way up a dogwood tree. The grapevines on the fence were thoroughly entwined in a climbing rosebush. On another part of the fence the honeysuckle was thriving—triumphant, even, over the poison ivy. A large bittersweet bush wound its tentacles around an old apple tree.

As I planned an evening of pruning, I made a few connections. Vines have a hard time living with other plants: They cling, they choke, they pursue their own growth. They compete with each other. Properly pruned, they can live and let live.

When we act like vines, we need to be pruned. But we get in trouble when we try to prune each other. What we need is a self-pruning mechanism, to check the urge to cling to or choke or dominate other life. If someone else tries to prune our needs and desires, it just doesn't work. If we can prune them for ourselves, then we understand better how the growth we cut back now yields a healthier relationship in the long run.

Mutual Love   Loving is more than compromise and trade-off; it is mutual nurturing of growth.

Loving is more than trust in each other; it is trust in something that transcends human expectation.

Love is the mutual gift of freedom with the mutual gift of commitment.

Love is more than being true to ourselves; it is being true to a common reverence for life and a common vision of community.

Love is more than loving each other; it is loving Life itself.

Aldous Huxley agreed with the biblical notion that "Love casts out fear." But, he added, "conversely, fear casts out love. . . ." Fear, he went on, also casts out intelligence, "casts out goodness, casts out all thoughts of beauty and truth."

Love Casts
Out Fear

In fear, we isolate ourselves.
In love, we connect with others.

In fear, we become immobilized.
In love, we are empowered to act.

In fear, we judge others.
In love, we seek justice.

In fear, we distrust.
In love, we trust.

In fear, we seek punishment.
In love, we seek mercy and forgiveness.

In fear, we see death.
In love, we see life.

In fear, we retreat.
In love, we reach out.

Let us respond to our times with love.
Let us reach out.

The Last Shall Be First

If there is one spiritual teaching common to all traditions, it must be that we have to lose ourselves in order to find ourselves. If we really want inner peace and purpose, we have to give up our need to succeed. In fact, we have to give up just about any need to be in control of our lives. The Taoist Lao Tse puts it this way:

Therefore the Sage puts himself last, and finds
    himself in the foremost place;
Regards his body as accidental,
    And his body is thereby preserved.
Is it not because he does not live for Self
    That his Self achieves perfection?

Paradoxically, when we let go of the need for power or recognition, we receive it, for we are in harmony instead of in contention with the natural creative principle of the universe. We give up our control and plug into a more natural process. As Chuang Tzu's millipede explains when it is asked how it moves all its legs: "Now all I do is put in motion the heavenly mechanism in me—I'm not aware of how the thing works."

The Taoist sage practices the virtue of "not contending":

The sage acts, but does not possess,
Accomplishes, but lays claim to no credit
Because [she] has no wish to seem superior.

I remember someone who drowned in a river as a hydraulic current drew him under. He drowned because he resisted. If he had moved with the flow of the water, it would have brought him back to the surface.

Think about this: A baby howls, yet its throat never gets hoarse; it makes fists without getting cramped fingers; it stares without blinking.

Or perhaps it is better not to think of it. For common to the sage and the child is the ability to lose the self in harmony with the Tao . . . without having to get it all figured out.

I have a magnet on my refrigerator that says, "Kids are people, too." It is there to remind me—I sometimes forget.

I expect the kids to leave me a note if they are going somewhere and to call if they will be late, but I sometimes forget to tell them where I have gone.

Sometimes I introduce myself to new families at church and forget to ask the names of the children.

Sometimes my level of sight looks straight ahead, over the heads of smaller children.

Kids are people, too. We talk about how important they are to our future, and say that they *are* the future. But they are not just future adults. They are people now, in the present. Children *are* the present.

Kids Are People, Too

What Are You Saving It For?

I was trying to write when my niece, who was getting ready to go back to college, interrupted me.

"Can I have this?" she said, holding up a rug that had been handed down in the family. "No," I said, "That is a genuine Navajo rug—it's very valuable. You don't put a rug like that on the floor."

"How about this?" she asked, displaying a large piece of material my husband had brought back for me from a trip to India. "It would look great on the couch."

"I really don't want that to be worn out," I said.

"Well, what about this?"

"You don't walk on a rug like that. . . ."

"And these?"

"You don't put old quilts like those on beds. . . ."

Finally she gave up. "Why do you just keep all these things stored away in a closet where no one can enjoy them?" she asked. "What are you saving them for?"

It was a good question. I thought of the unpolished silver and the glass objects safely shut away. I remembered my own sermon on gifts—about how the best gifts we receive are the ones we cannot keep. I made my point by burning a lovely candle that had been given to me. I watched it melt and I told the story of how the cat broke a little clay dog my father had given me, and how I cried. Then I talked about what was really important about the gift. It was a gift of memory—of my Great Dane, who liked to sit in people's laps, and slobbered all over the furniture. It was a gift of talent—the skills of an artist who could bring life to an image. It was a gift of time—time taken to shape something special from a lump of clay; time taken to wrap it carefully and mail it. And it was a gift of self. Memory, talent, time, self. . . none of these, I said in the sermon, broke when the cat sent the clay image crashing to the floor. It is dangerous, I said, to allow things to embody the sentiment that is precious to us.

"What are you saving it for?" The question stirs me. Those old things are valuable . . . but I don't plan to sell them. I am saving them for the sake of saving them— to hold onto something of the past.

My niece still needs an answer. I guess I will have to let her take one of those precious old things. And maybe, if she puts it away where it doesn't get too much use, she will still have it when one of her children asks her the same question.

For years I kept a check for $250 that was returned to me for nonpayment of funds. Account closed. Address unknown. I had not written down the number of a driver's license. I kept the check to remind me of how foolish I had been to trust a stranger.

On a recent visit to the library, I approached the librarian with an armful of books on Native American religion. As she stamped them, I reached for my card. "You won't need that today," she said. "Our computer is down." I wondered if she would ask me to write down my name and the titles of the books, but she didn't. I had an awkward feeling as I walked through the door with all those books; I might get fined if I brought them back late, but there would be no consequences if I did not bring them back at all. All day long, books were leaving the library and borrowers were trusted to return them.

That evening I went to pick up the carpet I had selected for my new office. I did not yet have a check from the church to pay for it, and explained to the salesperson that I did not have the money. Did he want me to pay for it myself, or should I pick it up in a few days? No, he said. Just take the carpet and send the check.

Twice in one day I was not asked for a driver's license and a major credit card. Not until I experienced all this trust in a single day did I think about how the attitude of distrust prevails in our everyday dealings with strangers.

Trust is hard to build. When it is broken, it is even more difficult to rebuild. Yet we know from our intimate relationships as well as our casual transactions with strangers that trust is essential to any community. No wonder we have so much trouble making treaties with foreign nations when we cannot even trust our own neighbors.

I have thrown away that check for $250. I may get taken again, but I would rather keep the memory of a day at the library and the carpet store to remind me of the hope that exists for community.

Walls

Something there is that doesn't love a wall.
—Robert Frost, "Mending Wall"

There is something in us that doesn't love a wall.
Yet we engage ourselves in building and repairing walls:

—walls between ourselves and strangers . . . ourselves
and our neighbors . . . ourselves and our friends . . .
ourselves and our families;

—walls of ignorance . . . stubbornness . . . prejudice . . .
apathy . . . fear . . . misunderstanding;

—walls that render us lonely and helpless,
—walls that defend us from the pain of loving,
—walls that protect us from the joy of living;

—walls that separate us from others,
—walls that separate us from ourselves.

May we be strengthened to tear down walls:

—to reach out to a stranger,
—to imagine an adversary's point of view,
—to see the familiar in the unfamiliar
  and the unfamiliar in the familiar.

May we engage those on the other side to help us tear
down walls and heal wounds.

May we touch and be touched by a power and a grace
that abide in the strength of our connections.

Amen.

Much Gesture, from the Pulpit—
Strong Hallelujahs roll—
Narcotics cannot still the Tooth
That nibbles at the soul—

Emily Dickinson wrote much about the burden of uncertainty that gnaws away at the consciousness of us mortal human beings. When I read these lines from Dickinson's poem, "The World Is Not Conclusion," I thought, "There's a sermon there somewhere." I was trying to figure out just where, when I remembered a conversation I had with a colleague.

All ministers really have only one sermon. So I asked my colleague what his sermon was.

"It's just one word," he said, "Live."

"Yeah," I said. "I suppose that's what mine is, too, except I would add, 'Live, in spite of. . . .'"

"In spite of what?" he asked.

"In spite of having to die, mainly. But there are other in-spite-ofs, too, like going to the dentist."

"Get serious," he said.

"I am serious. As far as I'm concerned, every dentist is Dr. Partridge, my childhood dentist. He didn't believe in Novocain. He liked to torture children. Going to the dentist means confronting Dr. Partridge—it means confronting fear."

"When's the last time you went to the dentist?" he asked, catching me off guard.

"What difference does that make?" I said.

"Well," he said, "if you live in spite of the pain and the fear of going to the dentist, does that mean that you go or that you avoid going?"

It was a theological question. It irritated me, but I got the point.

"So . . . ?" he persisted. "When's the last time you went to the dentist?"

"I don't have a dentist here," I said.

"You've lived here almost four years and you don't have a dentist?"

"I have good teeth," I said. "I brush them a lot."

Yes, all ministers have one sermon. And they preach it to themselves first.

"Chuck, come here!"

I was downstairs in the kitchen; Chuck was upstairs. He didn't question this unusual command, and promptly came down.

"Look!" I said, pointing to the corpse of a mouse.

We had given the mice full run of the house for some time, postponing the day when we would have to "do something" about them. We had even caught one alive while it was nibbling on leftover pizza and put it outside, hoping to avoid the unpleasant matter of extermination. But when I heard rustling in the boxes of notes and papers beneath my desk, I began having visions of my divinity school education being shredded into a theological nest. The decision was made.

"I feel so guilty," I said now, as we stood mournfully over our catch.

"Me, too," said Chuck, as he disposed of the evidence. Later he observed that I had artfully maneuvered the situation to avoid doing that myself.

After further discussion, we decided to get a cat.

It's a curious thing, conscience. To allow a cat to stalk our household pests was an acceptable solution—a form of violence that is part of nature's way. It seemed more humane than trapping or poisoning. But what about the cat who likes to play with its catch?

Getting a cat took the killing out of our hands, that's all.

Paradox We named the kitten Puppy Cat, which fits her contra-
dictory nature. She follows us around like a puppy.
With no apparent physical needs, she cries for attention. She just wants to chat, and demands some sign
that we are listening. If we try to pick her up, however,
she protests. "Keep close and pet me," she says, "but
don't hold me, I want to be free."

The needs for love and freedom create ambivalence in
most of us. Like Puppy Cat, we send out double
messages:

Love me . . . but do not intrude upon my space.
I want to be close . . . but I am afraid of being hurt.
I need you . . . but I want to be independent.
I need to be needed . . . but I don't want to be used.

And so on. We live on the boundary of so many inner
contradictions. We love the peacefulness of the country
. . . and the excitement of the city. We love the freshness
of a summer breeze . . . and the beauty of a winter storm.

You can create your own list. We are full of opposing
feelings and ideas. The trick is to be able to accept our
contradictions and keep them in balance, moving back
and forth between them rather than allowing them to
lock us in the uncertainty of ambivalence.

There's a difference between ambivalence and paradox.
In ambivalence, we are torn—our feelings conflict. In
paradox, we accept and admit our own tensions—our
feelings generate creative energy from the dynamic of
opposites. In ambivalence, we have difficulty making
commitments and decisions; we convey double messages to others. In paradox, we admit our uncertainties
and reservations and we act, wholeheartedly commit-
ting ourselves to our experiences.

Maybe the main difference is that in paradox we are
willing to make commitments when all we can ever
hope for is partial knowledge and uncertain outcome.

The summer was almost over and I would be back in the pulpit soon. I wanted some time to reflect and prepare, so I went to a cabin in the western hills of Connecticut for a few days. With enough food for a week and reading material for a month or two, I nestled into my woodsy retreat on Tuesday. By Friday I expected to turn out at least two sermons, and notes for a few more. I also hoped to pause for contemplation, walk in the woods, swim in the river, prepare delicious meals, and relax. And, oh yes—I took my jogging shoes.

Expectations

As I settled into the cabin, I spotted an intriguing novel. After stacking my books and papers onto a table, I began reading it. Later that evening I spoke with my husband Chuck.

"Have you gotten a lot of work done?" he asked.

"Well, I found this novel here. . . ."

"Novel?! You're supposed to be writing sermons!"

"Oh, there's probably some good sermon material in this novel."

On Friday morning, I packed up the items on the table. I smiled as I put the blank typing paper back in my briefcase. (Typing paper! Not only was I going to write the sermons, I was going to type them as well!) Nourished by solitude and sunsets, summer breezes and migrating geese, good food and a good novel, I returned home ready to begin a new year. Not ready in the way that I had hoped to be. I was ready because I let go of the expectations I had placed upon myself.

Most of the disappointments we experience are the result of expectations not met—expectations of ourselves, of situations, of other people. Perhaps we need solitude to re-examine and re-evaluate our expectations.

Each year I take some time for solitary retreat. I take fewer books, and I feel less guilty when I don't meet my expectations. But without fail I take more books than I will read.

Harvest

It had rained for three weeks. The hay, full of chiggers and ticks, was up to my armpits, except where it had fallen over and matted down. That was where the snakes were hiding. "I wish they would hurry up and cut the hay," I thought, "so I can walk through the meadow to the lake." I worried that what they would get when they mowed would all be gone to seed, and not fit for the horses to eat.

I was pretty excited when I heard the tractor coming down the road. "Oh, goody, goody!" I said aloud. (Yes, I really did say that.)

Then I thought about the flowers. With the late cutting, the Black-eyed Susans and the Queen Anne's Lace had hit their peak, and there was more of the precious orange Butterfly Weed than I had ever seen. I ran down to the field to gather a bouquet. Suddenly it seemed as if the meadow was nothing but wildflowers—especially Black-eyed Susans! As the sound of the tractor got louder, I was more aware of every golden bloom. I cut and cut, piling the meadow's treasure onto my arm. This is what people mean, I thought, when they talk about having a heightened awareness when they have a terminal illness or a brush with death. Forget the vases—it would take buckets to hold the bouquets I was gathering. As I returned to the house to put them in water, I felt a twinge for the thousands of flowers that awaited the blade.

Whoever coined the expression, "Make hay while the sun shines" probably didn't even cut hay. It was more likely someone who knew how flowers grow in a field when three weeks of rain come during the cutting season.

Gratitude

While I was gathering the flowers in the meadow, a neighbor shouted to me over the sound of the approaching tractor: "I saw the tractor coming and I picked a few myself. I hope you don't mind."

"Mind?" I said, "How can I mind? The wildflowers don't belong to me—they belong to God!"

I knew the neighbor's idea of God and mine wouldn't be at all the same, but he would know what I meant. When it comes to things like wildflowers, we all attend the same church.

My colleague Harry Meserve described as a pleasant surprise of advancing years the discovery of areas of knowledge, activity, and enjoyment that he had never before had time for or even considered. "This discovery," he writes, "reminds one that no matter how distinguished, competent, and successful we may have been . . . we are now as little children who must be taught from the start how to make our way in other fields of knowledge and activity. Such experience is good for the soul."

Aging is a lifelong process of adjustment to change. The people who age best are those who are granted serenity—as the famous prayer puts it—the serenity to accept the things they cannot change, the courage to change the things they can, and the wisdom to know the difference.

Getting older is one of those things that cannot be changed. The losses are different for different people. Sometimes the loss means giving up possessions to move into a smaller home, or giving up independence to move in with a family member. Or it may be the loss of physical abilities—hearing, walking, seeing. Gradually, age reminds us that we can't do things we used to do. Age forces us to redefine ourselves in terms of what we can do. It is an art to be able to grow through the losses and accept the process without giving in to a spirit of decline.

Aging is a process of growth, not of decline. I admire people who age well more than those who remain youthful. Sometimes it is hard to tell the difference, for both may appear vital and alert. But one avoids the realities of the autumn season of life by pretending that it's still summer, while the other enjoys the brilliant colors.

i who have died . . .

i who have died am alive again today. . . .
—e.e. cummings

The week before Easter, I was trying to write an Easter sermon. I had one uninspired paragraph. A colleague called, and I asked how his sabbatical was going. He had hiked through the bottom of the Grand Canyon and visited Native Americans and traveled up the Pacific coast to Big Sur. He told me that he had been born again.

"Don't worry," he added. "I haven't joined the fundamentalists. What I mean is I have a whole new way of looking at life. I came alive. I feel awake. I'm just not the same." He had also quit drinking. Alcohol was one of the things that had kept him from feeling fully alive.

What a great Easter story, I thought. But I was a bit jealous. There I sat in my study with books piled around me, trying to think of a new way to give the same old Easter message, and he was bursting with enthusiasm for life. Sometimes such enthusiasm is contagious, and sometimes it just makes us mad because we don't have it. After I hung up, wishing I could be born again, I went outside to get inspired by spring. First I noticed that the grass needed mowing and seeding. Then I spotted some trash in the azaleas. Then I checked to see how much my daffodils had come up in the last day. "Hurry up," I told them. "The ones at the church are way ahead of you."

I decided that if I tried to be born again right then it would be a premature birth. I went back to my books and papers. I learned one lesson about being born again: Don't try to force it. Be receptive. It will come.

Like the crocuses that push their way up through the hard earth to announce spring, our inner births have their own cycles. The same power that feeds the flower and gives us life is the spirit within that will be reborn again and again. The power waits, dormant to our senses, until the time is right.

36

Death and taxes. As the saying goes, these are the only things in life that we don't have any choice about. We can, however, file for extensions. Postponement gives us a little more time to get our act together.

Filing for an Extension

We opted for postponement when our dog was diagnosed with bone cancer. We had her leg amputated, knowing that she would live perhaps six months more. Then we prepared ourselves for the loss.

We don't always have the option of filing for an extension when it comes to facing death. Some of us will have time to prepare; others will be snatched away without warning. The important thing is to live so that death doesn't make us feel cheated. I remember the lines from *Hamlet*:

There is special providence in the fall of a sparrow.
If it be now, tis not to come;
if it be not to come, it will be now;
if it be not now, yet it will come.
The readiness is all.

The readiness is all. The readiness has more to do with life than death. It has to do with knowing that we have said what we need to say to people we love; it has to do with knowing we are doing more with our days than surviving; it has to do with acting upon our values now and not waiting for the day when we have more time. Yes, it has to do with life.

I am glad April 15 only happens once a year. Still, it isn't so bad to be reminded once a year to live in readiness for the time when we will not have the option of filing for an extension.

And when he drew near and saw the city he wept over it, saying, "Would that even today you knew the things that make for peace! But now they are hid from your eyes."

—Luke 19:41-42

Imagine how Palm Sunday might have been experienced by an average citizen living in Jerusalem. A ten-year-old, for example . . .

It was the Jerusalem tourist season. People were coming into town from all over for Passover week. Boy, did I hate the crowds! My folks owned an inn and all people did was complain about the straw in their mattresses. I went out on the edge of town to advertise for the inn, and I saw a bunch of people coming toward me all shouting and gathered around a colt. Then they took off some of their clothes (that's what really got my attention) and put them on the colt. I wasn't really surprised. Those country folks always act a little odd when they come to the city. Then they put a man on that little colt. I was worried the poor animal might collapse.

Then people started throwing more clothes and some tree branches in front of the man and they called him a king. "Hosanna in the highest!" they shouted. He looked about as much like a king as my little brother. And high is not what he was on that colt—his feet were almost dragging on the ground. I knew my parents would be furious, but I decided to get into the parade and see why this man was being called the messiah.

According to everything I had learned about the messiah, this guy did not make it. The messiah was supposed to be like David and Solomon. King David was a great warrior, a brave soldier. This man didn't even have a slingshot, as far as I could tell. And when someone made fun of him and threw a rock at him, he didn't say anything. I thought he was a real sissy, but then I followed the parade on into town where he went into the temple. Well, there was a big sale going on and he saw how some of the priests were overpricing stuff. He got real mad and said that they shouldn't be cheating people in God's house. He acted like he owned the place, which didn't go over too well with the priests. In fact, he made a real mess, turning some chairs and tables over. After that, the priests were out to get him, which was too bad, 'cause as far as I could tell, all he did was tell them not to cheat people in the temple.

One thing that was real obvious to me was that the people who put that man on the colt knew that he had some kind of power. You know, real power, like from God. And the priests knew it too, but they knew that his kind of power wouldn't go with their kind of power. Here he was with no horse and no weapons and no army, so his power wasn't like King David's. And he couldn't afford a place to stay in the city, so his power wasn't wealth like King Solomon's.

Some people say he will return again some day. But I bet they wouldn't recognize him if he did. Because he would still have the same kind of power. You'd think that with that kind of power, people would recognize him, but even the ones who say he was the messiah don't want to give up the kind of power that David and Solomon had.

Why is it that people say they want God's power, but when they experience it, they don't really want it after all?

The Music of the Earth

Let us listen to the music of the earth and offer a prayer of thanksgiving.

For the inspiration of winter's requiem, we give thanks.
For the renewal of spring's symphony, we give thanks.
For the lullabies of summer nights that cradle us in a vast
    universe, we give thanks.
For the oratorios of autumn that stir our restless spirits,
    we give thanks.

For the songs we sing together and the tunes that make
    us dance, and for the harmony of friendship, we
    give thanks.

We listen, too, for the discordant notes:
    —to the cries of children in nations where the sound
of gunfire masks the melodies of daily life;
    —to the harsh interruptions of illness that come too
soon for too many and isolate them from the music they
long to sing.

Learning to match our steps to the rhythm of the music
and the pace of others requires attention and devotion,
patience and willingness to falter.

We listen to the music of this earth, a blend of harmony
and discord. May it inspire us to compose beauty in our
lives and to join our voices with friends and strangers
alike.

Amen.

L'sho-noh ha-bo-oh bee-ru-sho-lo-yeem.   *Passover*

May Zion be blessed with peace, and may our brethren and
all humankind live in harmony and contentment.
Amen.
　　　　　—Benediction from the Passover Haggadah

The Jewish festival of Passover is known as "the Season
of Our Freedom." Recalling their ancestors' release from
bondage and oppression in Egypt, the people celebrate
liberation. As the earth is released from the grip of
winter, humanity celebrates release from bondage.

But the story doesn't stop with release. After terrible
plagues and the exodus from Egypt, Pharaoh's army
chased the people to the Red Sea, where the waters
parted for the Hebrews, then flowed back to swallow up
the Egyptian soldiers and their chariots.

Entering the wilderness, the people complained
("murmured") to Moses that it was his fault they were in
this awful place, hungry and tired and thirsty.

This was only the beginning. The people murmured a
lot in the wilderness. They recognized that bondage
had been pretty secure. Life in slavery was a drag, but at
least they knew what each day would bring, and a few
conveniences had made their burdens easier to bear.
Freedom sounded great when they were slaves, but now
that the people had to set up camp and find food in a
strange land, they weren't so sure.

It is safer to stay where things are familiar and events are
predictable. It is safer to be in bondage. Freedom means
risk; it means pursuing a dream of a promised land that
we may never reach. One Jewish legend tells that even
after Moses said words to part the sea, the waters did not
recede until the first Hebrew placed a foot in the water.

The Passover Seder is a thanksgiving meal—a time to
express gratitude to the God who hears the cries from all
who are oppressed and exploited. It is a time to express

regret for the suffering of all who pay the price for freedom, including those we call the enemy. And it is a time to express commitment to a vision of the promised land. For in the ritual of gratitude and remembering comes courage—the courage to put our feet in the water and take risks again and again for freedom.

There is incredible power in forgiveness. But forgiveness is not rational. One can seldom find a reason to forgive or be forgiven. Forgiveness is often undeserved. It may require a dimension of justice (penance, in traditional terms), but not always, for what it holds sacred is not fairness, but self-respect and community. Forgiveness does not wipe away guilt, but invites reconciliation. And it is as important to be able to forgive as it is to be forgiven.

Forgiveness

No, we do not forgive and forget. But when we invite the power of forgiveness, we release ourselves from some of the destructive hold the past has on us. Our hatred, our anger, our need to feel wronged—those will destroy us, whether a relationship is reconciled or not.

But we cannot just will ourselves to enter into forgiveness, either as givers or receivers. We can know it is right and that we want to do it and still not be able to.

We can, however, be open and receptive to the power of forgiveness, which, like any gift of the spirit, isn't of our own making. Its power is rooted in love. The Greek word for this kind of love is *agape*. Martin Luther King, Jr., defined *agape* as "Love seeking to preserve and create community." This kind of love is human, but it is also the grace of a transcendent power that lifts us out of ourselves. It transforms and heals; and even when we are separated by time or space or death, it reconciles us to ourselves and to Life. For its power abides not just between us but within us. If we invited the power of *agape* to heal our personal wounds and give us the gift of forgiveness, we would give our world a better chance of survival.

Love Renewing   Spirit of Life, fill our hearts and cleanse us.
Remove the resentments that create walls between us.
Remove the jealousies that make us small.
Remove the fears and guilts that close us into ourselves.

Cleanse us and empty us of these things so that we may
know the force and power and fullness of the love that
reconciles us to ourselves, to one another, and to Life.

Give us in these moments of quiet the power of love that
forgives

—that forgives us when we fail ourselves
—that allows us to ask for forgiveness
—that empowers us to forgive.

With forgiveness, lift us into new ways of loving; free us
to care

—to care for ourselves
—to care for our families
—to care for our friends
—to care for strangers.

With caring, open us to new ways of giving. Free us to
give

—to give our time
—to give our affection
—to give our affirmation
—to give ourselves.

Grateful for the love that nourishes us, we celebrate its
power to renew us, to change us, and to give us hope.

Amen.

Eli Eli lema sabachthani.
　　—Matthew 27:46

"My God, My God, why hast thou forsaken me?" Jesus cried out these words in his own language, Aramaic. This is one of only a few places in the gospels where Jesus' own language is preserved.　Strong words. Memorable words.

Jesus was alone. Judas had betrayed him; the disciples had disappeared; and Peter—the faithful Peter who would become the foundation of the church—denied knowing him. At this moment of deepest need, God had run out on him too. Jesus was alone.

Some time ago, I sat by the bedside of a woman who was forty-five and dying painfully of cancer. She had a lot more living to do. But each day, more life slipped away, and she wailed. Not cried. Not wept.　She *wailed* through the agony—a wail of despair that defies translation. Here was a highly successful woman. She was loved dearly by family and friends. But in her dying, she was alone. And so she prayed; she cried out wordlessly to the absent God.

This is the paradox. In our despair, we are moved to pray, even if our prayer is no more than a cry of rage against the forces of life in which we have placed our trust. In suffering, like Jesus, we feel alone and forsaken. But in suffering we turn to the absent God, and in our inarticulate utterings, declare God to be present.

That does not mean that we feel the presence; it does not insure that there is a presence; it only insists that deep in the empty soul full of absence, a wail is addressed to God and no one but God understands it because no one else knows the language.

The Growing
Season

"I am not religious," says my neighbor, as he hoes the rows between his beans and corn.

"Oh yes, you are," I say to myself.

To plant a seed is an act of faith.
To collect compost is a response of gratitude to the creator.
To water, fertilize, and mulch the ground is an expression of religious responsibility.
To kneel down and pull weeds is a prayer.
To harvest is to participate in the fullness and grace of the spirit.
To protect and replenish creation is to love God.

"I am not religious," says my neighbor.

Yes, you are, I say.

The resurrection isn't the only supernatural event in the Easter story. The disciples of Jesus lived in a world of the supernatural. According to Matthew, when Jesus died, the earth shook and coughed up corpses all over and "many bodies of the saints who had fallen asleep were raised." After the resurrection of Jesus, these saints showed up in Jerusalem. Well, if just by dying Jesus could empty all those tombs, maybe his own empty tomb was no marvel.

No, in a world where spirits rose up on a regular basis, there had to be something more special going on than just another corpse walking about. This was a resurrection of many souls, not from death, but from deadness.

What do I mean by deadness? I mean the things inside that kept the disciples away from Jesus' funeral—fear, cowardice, lack of conviction and purpose. And I mean those same things in our own lives that prevent us from feeling alive—things like fear, cowardice, and lack of conviction and purpose. And things like the loneliness, grief, and boredom that numb us to life.

It's as if we let parts of ourselves die and stuff them away in a tomb of the soul. Sometimes that tomb is not such a bad place. It is like a womb—safe and secure, comfortable and predictable. Our tomb-life may be nothing more than the safety and comfort of a nice predictable routine. Or it may be a shelter from the world and its problems—a place to hide from the Jesus who called for a world where people care for one another. Whether it is escape or comfort, the time comes for us to roll away the stone and come out.

Rolling Away the Stone

In the tomb of the soul, we carry secret yearnings, pains, frustrations, loneliness, fears, regrets, worries.

In the tomb of the soul, we take refuge from the world and its heaviness.

In the tomb of the soul, we wrap ourselves in the security of darkness.

Sometimes this is a comfort. Sometimes it is an escape.

Sometimes it prepares us for experience. Sometimes it insulates us from life.

Sometimes this tomb-life gives us time to feel the pain of the world and reach out to heal others. Sometimes it numbs us and locks us up with our own concerns.

In this season where light and dark balance the day, we seek balance for ourselves.

Grateful for the darkness that has nourished us, we push away the stone and invite the light to awaken us to the possibilities within us and among us—possibilities for new life in ourselves and in our world.

Amen.

We receive fragments of holiness, glimpses of eternity, brief moments of insight. Let us gather them up for the precious gifts that they are, and, renewed by their grace, move boldly into the unknown.

Benediction